# READ, WRITE, AND

## A Bug in a Jug
and Other Funny Rhymes

## Hattie and the Fox

Donna Alvermann
Connie A. Bridge
Barbara A. Schmidt
Lyndon W. Searfoss
Peter Winograd
Scott G. Paris

**D.C. Heath and Company**
HEATH Lexington, Massachusetts/Toronto, Ontario

## Acknowledgments

*Editorial* **Director of Reading:** Tina Miller. **Managing Editor:** Kathleen T. Migdal. **Supervising Editor:** Susan D. Paro.
*Production Coordinator:* Bryan Quible.
*Project Development:* Brown Publishing Network, Inc.

**Illustration** **3:** Sylvie Wickstrom. **4:** Daniel Moreton. **5-8:** Stephan Geissbuhler. **9:** Sylvie Wickstrom. **10-12:** Daniel Moreton. **13-16:** Steve Bjorkman. **17:** Ajin Noda. **18:** Sylvie Wickstrom. **19-22:** Renee Williams. **23-26:** Ajin Noda. **27-30:** James Marshall. **31, 32:** Ajin Noda. **33-34:** Mary Jo Mazzella. **35-36:** Mary Thelen. **37-40:** Loretta Lustig. **41:** Susan Unger. **42:** John Himmelman. **43:** Mary Jo Mazzella. **44:** John Himmelman. **45-48:** James Marshall. **49-50:** Susan Unger. **51:** Pat Wong. **52:** Andrea Tachierd. **53-56:** Hilda Offen. **57-60:** James Marshall. **61:** Pat Wong. **61-62:** Susan Unger.

International Standard Book Number: 0–669–30214–7

11 12 13–POO–99

Name . . . . . . . . . . . . . . . . . . . . . . . . . . . . . . . . . . . . . . . . . . . . . . . . . . . . . . . . .

tree

log

_____

\_ \_ \_ \_ \_ \_ \_ \_ \_ \_ \_ \_ \_ \_ \_

_____

bug

hat

_____

\_ \_ \_ \_ \_ \_ \_ \_ \_ \_ \_ \_ \_ \_ \_

_____

house

_____

\_ \_ \_ \_ \_ \_ \_ \_ \_ \_ \_ \_ \_ \_ \_

_____

**Directions:** Have children write their favorite rhyming word for each picture. Remind them to use their word cards for help.

_____
- - - - - - - at

_____
- - - - - - - at

_____
- - - - - - - at

_____
- - - - - - - at

_____
- - - - - - - at

_____
- - - - - - - at

**Directions:** Children write letters to make words that end in **-at**. Then they draw a picture for each word they make.

**Recognizing short vowel a**

# Come with Me

This is Mr. Bee in the tree.

8

Meet Mrs. Mouse.
Meet Mr. Frog.
Meet Mr. Bee.

2

Here is Mr. Bee.
He is going to the tree.

7

Here is Mrs. Mouse.
She is going to her house.

3

This is Mr. Frog in the bog.

6

This is Mrs. Mouse in her house.

4

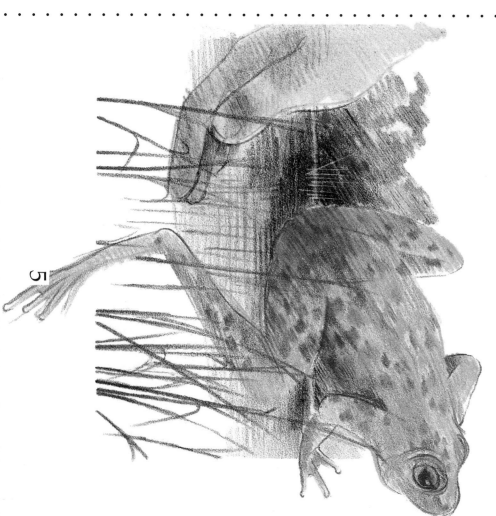

Here is Mr. Frog.
He is going to the bog.

5

Name . . . . . . . . . . . . . . . . . . . . . . . . . . . . . . . . . . . . . . . . . . . . . . . . . . . . . . . . . . . . . . . . . . . .

_____

_ _ _ _ _ _ _ _ _

This is a _____ .

_____

_ _ _ _ _ _ _ _ _

This is a _____ .

_____

_ _ _ _ _ _ _

_____

_ _ _ _ _ _ _

This is the _____ in the _____ .

_____

**Directions:** Children write the names of the pictures to complete the sentences.

The _____ is in the _____ .

The _____ is on the _____ .

**Directions:** Children use rhyming words to complete each sentence. Then children draw a picture to show what the sentence means.

Name . . . . . . . . . . . . . . . . . . . . . . . . . . . . . . . . . . . . . . . . . . . . . .

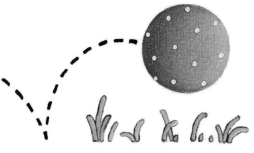

The ball is <u>up</u>.                    The ball is <u>down</u>.

The ball is <u>on</u> the rug.        The ball is <u>off</u> the rug.

The ball is <u>in</u>.                    The ball is <u>out</u>.

**Directions:** Children draw pictures to illustrate the words that have opposite meanings. Then children cut out the sections, tape them together as a circle, and wear it as a hat.

**Understanding antonyms**

Understanding antonyms

# Doing the Huggy Buggy

Doing the Huggy Buggy.

How do you do the Huggy Buggy?

Read these steps.

You put your arm in.
You take your arm out.

Can you do the Huggy Buggy now?

Try it.

Then you hug a friend
And turn yourself about.

3

Last, you jump in.
Next you jump out.

Then you hug a friend
And turn yourself about.

6

You put your hands in.
You take your hands out.

Then you hug a friend
And turn yourself about.

4

You put your head in.
You take your head out.

Then you hug a friend
And turn yourself about.

5

# My Friend

**Directions:** Children draw a picture and write about a friend.

**Writing about a friend**

Name . . . . . . . . . . . . . . . . . . . . . . . . . . . . . . . . . . . . . . . . . . . . . . . . . . . . . . . . . . . . . . . . . . . . .

Where did the little dog go?

_____

- - - - - - - - - - - - - - - - - - - - - - - - - - - - - - - - - - -

_____

- - - - - - - - - - - - - - - - - - - - - - - - - - - - - - - - - - -

_____

- - - - - - - - - - - - - - - - - - - - - - - - - - - - - - - - - - -

_____

**Directions:** Children draw the little lost dog. Then they write the answer to the question.

Writing story ideas

What will Nat do?

Who ate this cake?

2

Who did it?

You know who.

My dog.

7

Who chased my cat up the tree?

3

Who buried the bone?

6

Who knocked down the jug?

4

Who messed up the wash?

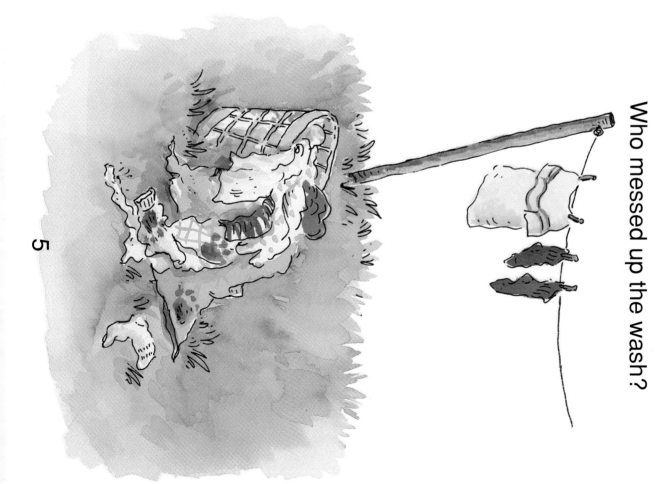

5

# Four Little Monkeys

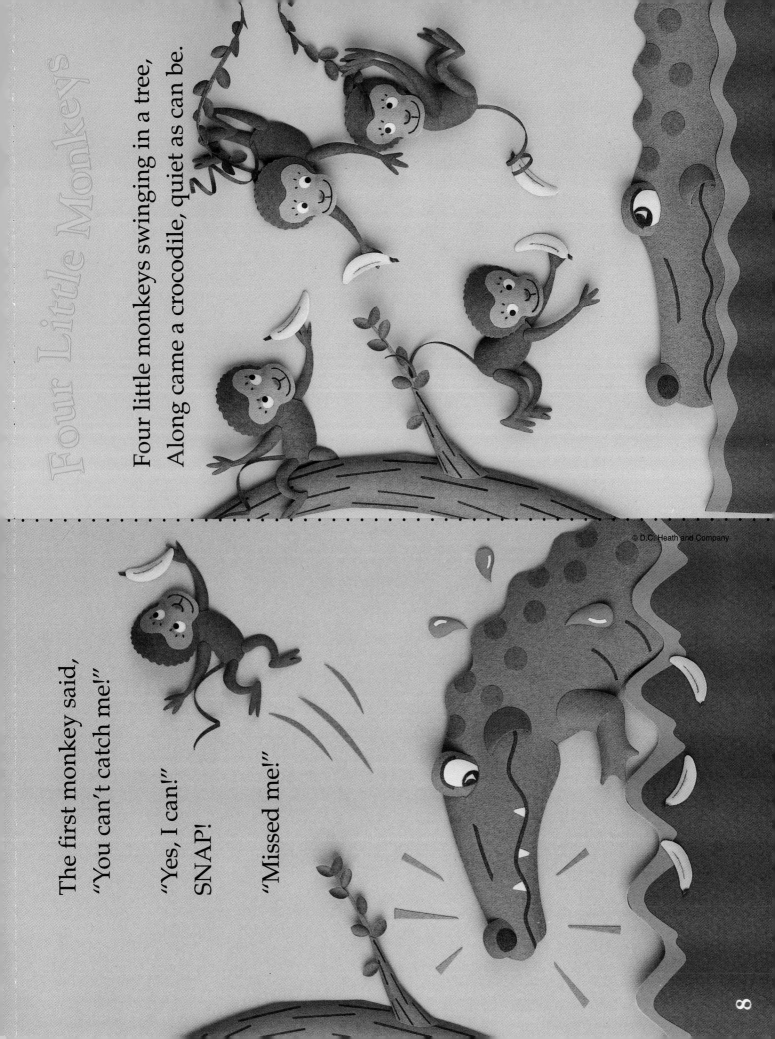

Four little monkeys swinging in a tree,
Along came a crocodile, quiet as can be.

The first monkey said,
"You can't catch me!"

"Yes, I can!"
SNAP!

"Missed me!"

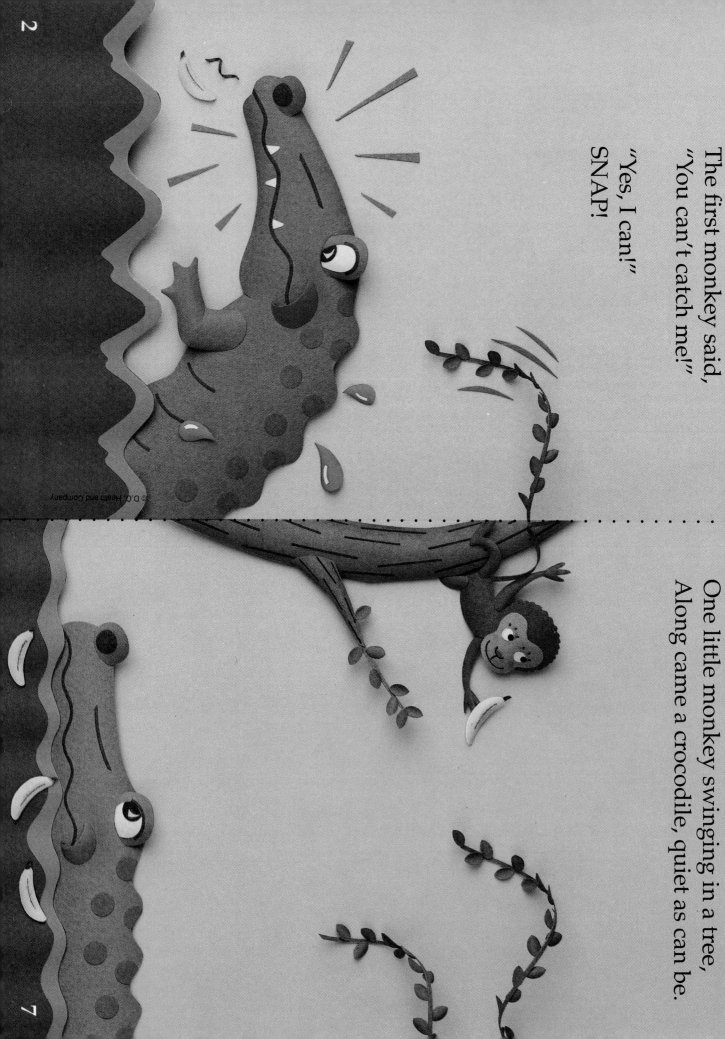

The first monkey said,
"You can't catch me!"

"Yes, I can!"
SNAP!

One little monkey swinging in a tree,
Along came a crocodile, quiet as can be.

Three little monkeys swinging in a tree,
Along came a crocodile, quiet as can be.

The first monkey said,
"You can't catch me!"

"Yes, I can!"
SNAP!

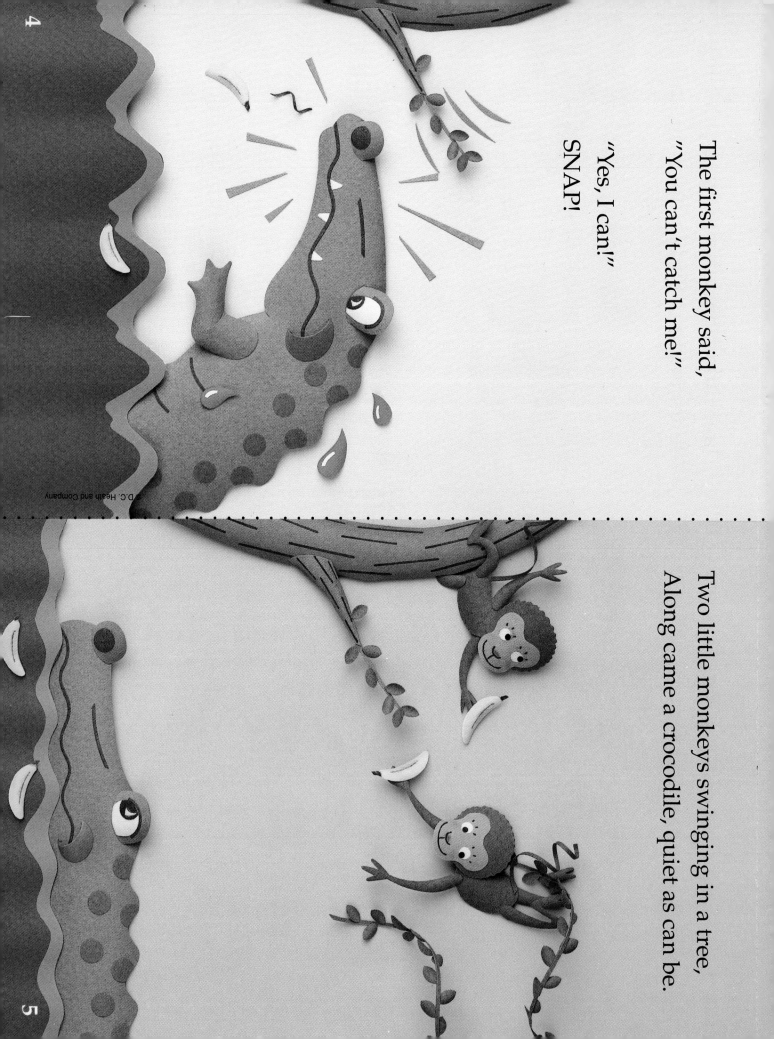

The first monkey said,
"You can't catch me!"
"Yes, I can!"
SNAP!

Two little monkeys swinging in a tree,
Along came a crocodile, quiet as can be.

4

5

# The New Hat

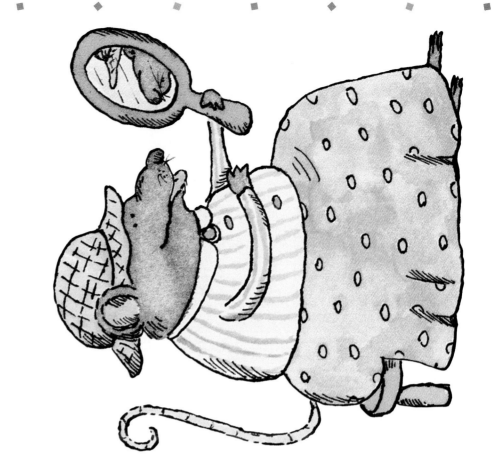

The horse ate the hat.

"Yes, I do like your hat!" said the horse.

8

A rat made a new hat.

"I like my hat," she said.
"Now I will go out."

2

"Hello. Do you like my new hat?"
said the rat.

7

"Hello. Do you like my new hat?"
said the rat.

"Yes, but put this on it,"
said the dog.

3

"Hello. Do you like my new hat?"
said the rat.

"Yes, but put this on it,"
said the fish.

6

"Hello. Do you like my new hat?"
said the rat.

"Yes, but put this on it,"
said the bird.

4

"Hello. Do you like my new hat?"
said the rat.

"Yes, but put this on it,"
said the cat.

5

Name . . . . . . . . . . . . . . . . . . . . . . . . . . . . . . . . . . . . . . . . . . . . . . . . . . . . . . . . . . . . . . . . . . . . .

**Directions:** Children write about a cat and draw a picture. Have them give their cat a name.

Name . . . . . . . . . . . . . . . . . . . . . . . . . . . . . . . . . . . . . . . . . . . . . . . . . . . . . . . . . . . . . . . . . . . . . . . . . . . . . .

I liked _____

_____ .

I liked it because _____

_____ .

**Directions:** Children write the name of the chant, book, story, or rhyme they liked best. Then they draw a picture to go with their writing.

32    A BUG IN A JUG • Lesson 8

**Writing a review**

Name ................................................................................

**Directions:** Have the children write what they know about a hen.

Name ...........................................................................................................

**Directions:** Have the children write what they know about a fox.

HATTIE AND THE FOX • Lesson 1

**Writing about a fox**

**Directions:** Children color in the fox, cut it out, and use it to retell the story.

# Four Hens

"What do you see?" said Rooster.

"I see four hens," said Fox.
"I see four hens for me."

Rooster and hen flew up to the tree.

Fox looked up.
He said, "There are no hens for me."

8

"Cock-a-doodle-doo.
Cock-a-doodle-doo," said Rooster.
"It's the fox!"

2

"What do you see?" said Rooster.
"I see one hen," said Fox.
"I see one hen for me."

7

One hen flew away.
Then there were three.

3

Two hens flew away.
Then there was one.

6

"What do you see?" said Rooster.
"I see three hens," said Fox.
"I see three hens for me."

4

"Cock-a-doodle-doo.
Cock-a-doodle-doo.
Look out!" said Rooster.
"It's the fox!"

5

Name . . . . . . . . . . . . . . . . . . . . . . . . . . . . . . . . . . . . . . . . . . . . . . . . . . . . . . . . . . . . . . . . . . . . . . . . . . . . . . . . .

I can see _____ .
_____

**Directions:** Have children draw a picture of what they can see. Then write a sentence about it.

**Writing a sentence**

Name . . . . . . . . . . . . . . . . . . . . . . . . . . . . . . . . . . . . . . . . . . . . . . . . . . . . . . . . . . . . . . . . . . . . . . .

**Directions:** Children write the word that names the picture. Later, they write some words that rhyme with the words on this page.

42    HATTIE AND THE FOX • Lesson 3                                   **Writing words with short vowel** a

Name . . . . . . . . . . . . . . . . . . . . . . . . . . . . . . . . . . . . . . . . . . . . . . . . . . . . . . . . . . . . . . . . . . . . . . . .

## What did that animal say to Hattie?

_____

- - - - - - - - - - - - - - - - - - - - - - - - - - - - - - - -

_____

- - - - - - - - - - - - - - - - - - - - - - - - - - - - - - - -

_____

- - - - - - - - - - - - - - - - - - - - - - - - - - - - - - - -

_____

- - - - - - - - - - - - - - - - - - - - - - - - - - - - - - - - .

_____

**Directions:** Children draw the animal and then write what the animal said to Hattie.

**Writing what an animal said**

HATTIE AND THE FOX • Lesson 3   43

Name . . . . . . . . . . . . . . . . . . . . . . . . . . . . . . . . . . . . . . . . . . . . . . . . . . . . . . . . . . . . . . . . . . . . . . . .

**Directions:** Have children look at the pictures. Then have them draw a picture of what will happen next and write about it.

**Predicting outcomes**

"Here comes Pig,"
said Rabbit.

"Oh no! Look at Pig!"
said Frog.

"Pig!" said Pig.

"Oh my!" said Frog.
"We did not know it was you!"

"Good for Pig!" said Rabbit.
"Good for Pig!"

8

"Hello, Pig," said Rabbit.

"Good to see you, Pig," said Frog.

2

"No," said Rabbit.
"Pig is not that tall."

"Who is it?" said Frog.

7

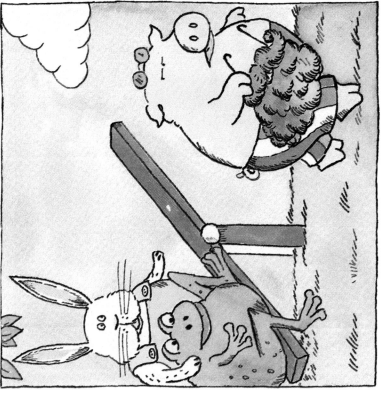

"Rats," said Pig.
"How did you know who I was?"

"We just did," said Frog.

3

"Look!" said Rabbit.
"Who is that?"

"It is not Pig," said Frog.

6

"Look!" said Rabbit.
"Here comes Pig."

"Hello, Pig," said Frog.
"Good to see you."

4

"How did you know who I was?"
said Pig.

"We just did," said Frog.
"We just did."

5

Name . . . . . . . . . . . . . . . . . . . . . . . . . . . . . . . . . . . . . . . . . . . . . . . . . . . . . . . . . . . . . . . . . .

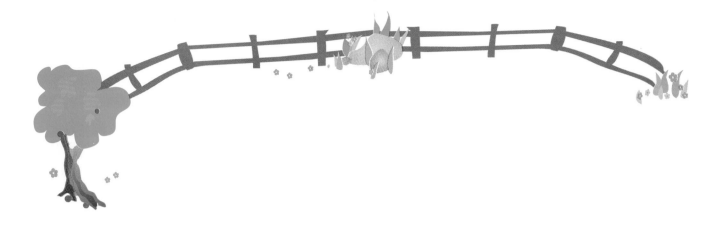

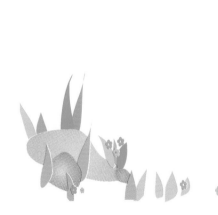

This little pig _____

_____

_____

_____ .

_____

**Directions:** Children draw a picture of a pig. Then they write a sentence about the pig.

# An Animal Story

## Who?

_____

- - - - - - - - - - - - - -

_____

- - - - - - - - - - - - - -

_____

## Where?

_____

- - - - - - - - - - - - - -

_____

- - - - - - - - - - - - - -

_____

## What happens?

_____

- - - - - - - - - - - - - - - - - - - - - - - - - - - - - - - - - - - -

_____

_____

- - - - - - - - - - - - - - - - - - - - - - - - - - - - - - - - - - - -

_____

_____

- - - - - - - - - - - - - - - - - - - - - - - - - - - - - - - - - - - -

_____

**Directions:** Children write ideas for an animal story by answering each question.

Name . . . . . . . . . . . . . . . . . . . . . . . . . . . . . . . . . . . . . . . . . . . . . . . . . . . . . . . . . . . . . . . .

"Good grief!"

_____

— — — — — — — — — — — — — — — —

_____ .

"Well, well!"

_____

— — — — — — — — — — — — — — — —

_____ .

"Who cares?"

_____

— — — — — — — — — — — — — — — —

_____ .

"So what?"

_____

— — — — — — — — — — — — — — — —

_____ .

"What next?"

_____

— — — — — — — — — — — — — — — —

_____ .

**Directions:** Children finish each sentence by writing the correct "said" phrase on the line. Then they match the sentences to the sentences in the story.

**Identifying the speaker**

Name . . . . . . . . . . . . . . . . . . . . . . . . . . . . . . . . . . . . . . . . . . . . . . . . . . . . . . . . . . . . . . . . . . . . . . .

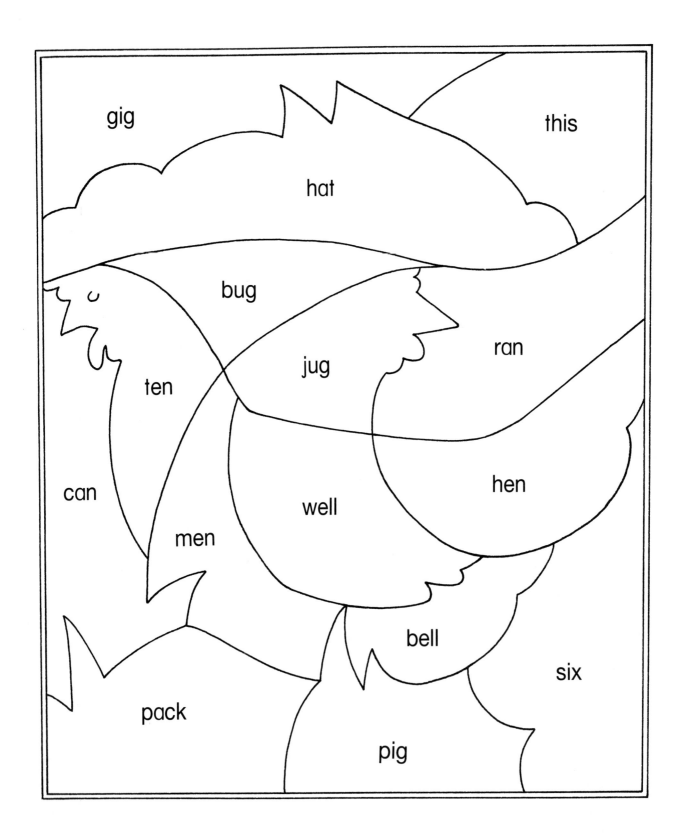

gig

this

hat

bug

jug

ran

ten

can

hen

well

men

bell

six

pack

pig

**Directions:** Children find the short **e** words in the puzzle and color in those parts to find the hidden picture. Later, they find the rhyming words, such as **bug** and **jug**.

# Goose on the Loose

"Oh, no!" said the cow.
"The goose is on the loose!"

Down went the goose.
She is not on the loose.

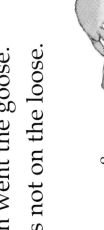

8

"Help, help," said the pig.
"Get the goose.
It's on the loose."

2

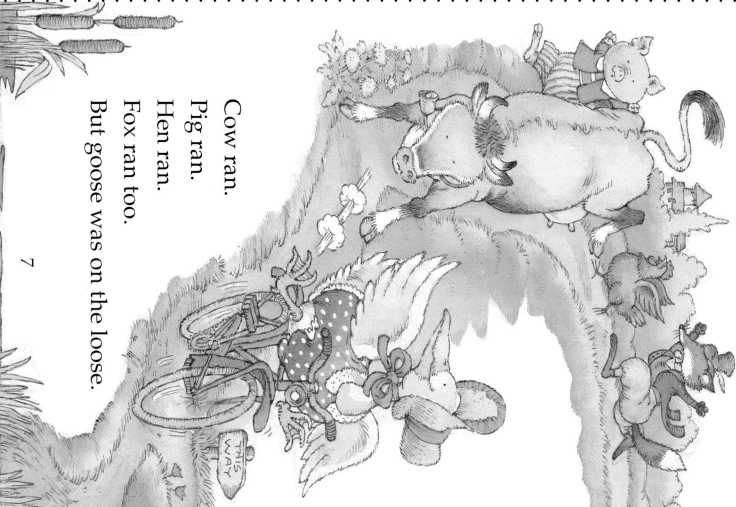

Cow ran.
Pig ran.
Hen ran.
Fox ran too.
But goose was on the loose.

7

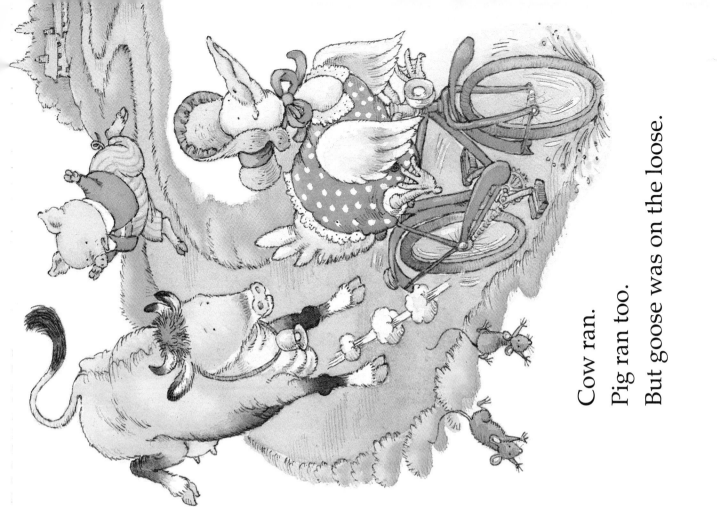

Cow ran.
Pig ran too.
But goose was on the loose.

3

"What is that?" said the fox.

"It's on the loose.
Let's get the goose."

6

"It's the goose," said the hen.
"It's on the loose.
Let's get the goose."

4

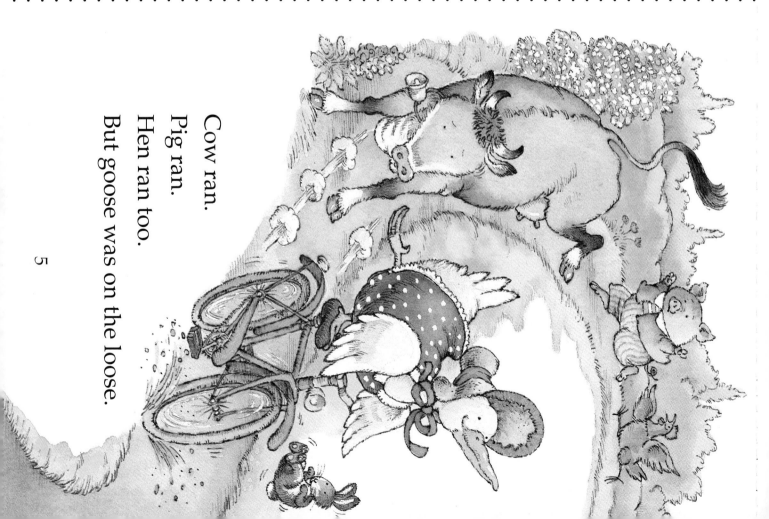

Cow ran.
Pig ran.
Hen ran too.
But goose was on the loose.

5

# I See You!

"I see you!" said the bird.
"I see you, rabbit!"

"Go home," said the rabbit.
"I have to sleep."

2

© D.C. Heath and Company

The fox ran home.

"Do I have to go home?"
said the bird.

"No," said the rabbit and the duck.
"We need you!"

7

"I see you!" said the bird.
"I see you, duck!"

"Go home," said the duck.
"I have to read."

3

"A fox!" said the rabbit.

"Run!" said the duck.

The rabbit and the duck ran home.

This made the fox mad.

6

"This bird may not stay,"
said the rabbit.

"No," said the duck.

4

"I see you!" said the bird.
"I see you, fox!"

"Go home," said the fox.
"I have to eat."

5

Name . . . . . . . . . . . . . . . . . . . . . . . . . . . . . . . . . . . . . . . . . . . . . . . . . . . . . . . . . . . . . . . .

Sequencing story events

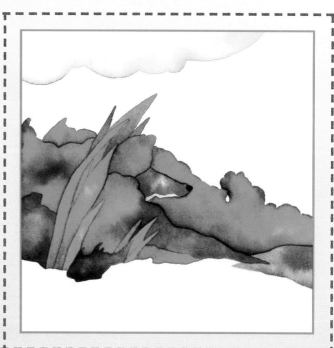

**Directions:** Cut out the pictures and paste them down to show the order in which Hattie saw the fox. Use the pictures to retell the story.

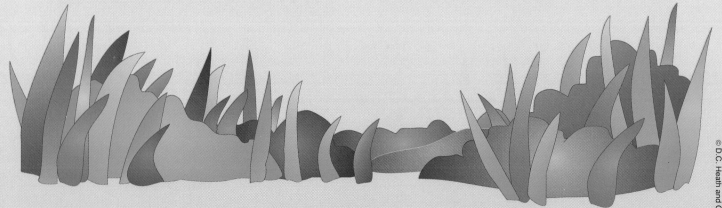

Name . . . . . . . . . . . . . . . . . . . . . . . . . . . . . . . . . . . . . . . . . . . . . . . . . . . . . . . . . .

Look what
I can do.

I can

_____

_ _ _ _ _ _ _ _ _ _ _ _ _ _ _ !

_____

**Directions:** Have the children write a word to complete the sentence. Then have them cut out, color, and decorate their certificate in any way they wish.